FOREWORDS:
This book is a continuation of self-made writer Freddie L Sirmans Sr. Previous book "Cold Steel Raw Truth About White Liberals & Race In America." Freddie L Sirmans Sr. is not educated and don't pretend to be, but he has one of the deepest and penetrating economic minds that exist today. His writing is raw, crude, and unabashed, you read at you own risk if you can take his bitter word medicine. Not everyone can take more than a page or so before dismissing him as a cold uncaring throwback to a distance era. However, he feels his writing is a calling or destiny duty and he must sound the distress call alarm for the survival of his beloved homeland. Come hell or high waters he feels he must keep sounding the distress alarm as long as breath is left in his body. He views himself as a neurotic mentally handicapped cripple; still, duty honor country comes first with him. He believes to try and keep trying is the greatest of all virtues.

MEASLES VACCINE DISCUSSION

INJECTION: SIRMANS LOG: 05 FEBRUARY 2015, 0020 HOUR

I decided to throw my two cents worth in on this measles vaccine discussion going around: Vitamin B-6 cured my carpal tunnel problems, but the testing science says that is a myth and taking vitamin B-6 had nothing to do with it.

So, when I hear all of these people claiming they noticed the difference right after the vaccine I'm not one to totally dismiss their claims no matter what the supposedly science says. Sure, I believe all vaccines are safe and should be taken.

However, I do have a problem with taking more than one vaccine at a time to save time and labor cost. I think if there is a problem that would be where it lies. I think no vaccine should be give within three months from the last one.

The totally ignored fact is none of this epidemic of diseases would be happening if not for the USA government allowing floods of illegal children in without first being tested or

quarantined, Duh.
INJECTION END

I'm going out on a limb and admit to a personal belief. I think the executive branch of government has been allowed to operate out of control ever since the days of Richard M Nixon. Nixon was the first president to go hog wild and start enacting all of these so-called federal environmental laws, safety laws, affirmative action laws, and other such executive only laws.

Sure, it was seen as a good thing, but the flaw in allowing one man the power to wield so much power is sooner or later it may lead to rewarding political friends and punishing political enemies. I think we have now arrived to an imperial presidency and there is not a thing politically we the people can do to put a stop to it.

The first thing is we the people don't have the will to stop anything because we as a people are morally and spiritual bankrupt. The second thing is we the people have surrendered our

God given family provider role for the most part to a super all powerful welfare state beast. It is a fact whoever is the provider is the boss and you have no choice but to dance to his/her tune.

The almost 200 years before our liberal induced "New deal" hardly anyone was dependent on the government for anything. Sure, as a last resort I feel the government must come to the aid of the people, but never more than on a temporary basis. Right now in a showdown and it may come to that, the states will lose and end up as just federal districts.

The states stupidly voluntarily piss away their real power, now no state governor or legislature appoints and controls its two senators. And, in my view technically speaking United State Senators operate more like independent state agents and are scared to death of special interest groups. Yet, all is not lost.

A genuine true free market place economy is the most powerful thing on

earth and will trump even our welfare state beast led by a modern imperial presidency. All the USA need to do to survive is return to a 1937 style economy. The evil 1938 socialist minimum wage law came along and castrated the USA economy.

Any wage or price control destroys a free market place economy's ability to discipline itself, which is its power and greatest asset. So, as you can see only a miracle can save the USA. We have an almost total economically ignorant mass news media and general public to bat that don't know a business can't exist without making a profit, duh.

Most of the world is poor and will always be poor simply because their governments won't allow proprietors to keep more of their profit. I think the USA has two choices in terms of survival, either we repeal or eliminate the 1938 minimum wage law entirely, or hope we survive a total economic collapse, which could be sooner than later.

Folks, I'm a raw crude self-made

writer, I know some of my word medicine is bitter to swallow. I say get over it, our survival is at stake, and you can take that to the bank.

Folks, here it is in a nutshell, our nation somehow either gets rid of the evil 1938 socialist minimum wage law or the nation perishes, period.

All of this other stuff I hear everyday like changing the tax system and countless other tinkering here or tinkering there is like nipping at someone's heel or pissing on a barn fire expecting to put it out. Duh.

The conservatives and tea party members are advocating balancing the national budget and cutting out tax wasting social programs. Sure, that would have been wise eighty or so years ago but today it is like spitting into the wind. All that will do is make the beast angrier and the advocates will be booted out of office.

Our welfare state beast now is much too powerful to be brought under control by any such feeble fine tuning or manipulation today. There is only one force in existence powerful enough to take down this out of control welfare state beast and save the last bastion of true individual freedom left in the world today.

That force is a genuine true free market place economy. But, there exist a huge problem here; a genuine true free market place economy cannot exist if any kind of wage or price control is in place. What the USA has today is a phony P…. of an economy with no power to discipline itself or the county.

No economic discipline is why our culture, morals, and religious structure are shot all to hell. In term of raw survival we have almost no tools left to stay the course. I'm referring to tools like a strong nuclear and extended family system, or enough small farmers and home gardeners for bartering capacity to buy time when this phony economy soon collapses.

The fact is the 1938 federal minimum wage law must be repealed or eliminated entirely before a genuine true free market place economy can save the USA. And the chance of that ever happening seems to be zero to none. So, unless a miracle happens we will just ride out this big phony p.... of an economy until it collapses and sends us all back to the Stone Age.

I predict right now some western nations are searching for the right language to quietly neutralize any wage or price controls. We are on a merry go-round to doom and anyone with an ounce of economic wisdom knows it.

Cut the 1938 minimum wage chain and sic the all power free market place attack dog on this evil tax grubbing welfare state beast, sic-um, sic-um boy.

Ever since the "New deal" the shallow minded liberals and democrats have had this great country by the balls. And there is only one force on earth powerful enough to break their grip. That force is a genuine true free market economy. Otherwise, our greedy tax grubbing welfare state beast is going to finally figure out a way to a seize our guns.

And if you don't think at some point our docile humble welfare state beast won't go door to door seizing guns you don't know history. Plus, with today's technology don't ever think they can't find them.

Our armed populace is the last defense saving the last bastion of true individual freedom left in the world today. And our slobbering tax grubbing welfare state beast with an insatiable apatite feels one way or another the guns must go.

SIRMANS LOG: 29 JANUARY 2015, 2048 HOURS

INJECTION ABOUT THIS FOOTBALL DEFLATION MADNESS THING: SIRMANS LOG: 23 JANUARY 2015, 1923 HOURS
Obamacare is about to collapse this whole USA economy and the entire national liberal news media's only concern is the weight of a pig skin.

Today we have turned into a nation of people with extremely weak to nonexistence survival instincts.

We couldn't recognize a moral or physical threat if it slapped us upside the head. And I blame it all on our liberal induced welfare state. Besides, it shouldn't be that hard to isolate who tampered with the footballs air pressure in the first place.

The first thing is there are cameras all over the place. The second thing is most likely there was always more than one person within sight of the footballs at all times. And The third thing is give everyone with a reason to be near the footballs a lie detector test.

That being said, I think the whole thing equals making a mountain out of a mole hill.
PS: I'm paraphrasing, but, I think it was Vince Lombardi who said, "Winning ain't everything it's the only thing."
INJECTION END

COMING OBAMACARE DESTRUCTION INJECTION: SIRMANS LOG: 23 JANUARY 2015, 1515 HOURS.

I THINK BY APRIL 15TH PLUS 30 DAYS WE WILL HEAR THE FIRST RUMBLINGS COMING FROM THE ECONOMIC VOLCANIC ERUPTION THAT MAY LEAD TO A TOTALLY USA ECONOMY COLLAPSE. WE'LL SEE, THE WAIT WON'T BE MUCH LONGER. **INJECTION END.**

IDEOLOGY INJECTION: SIRMANS LOG: 21 JANUARY 2015, 1249 HOURS

I have never in my life advocated for a lower minimum wage because that is even more sinister than a higher minimum wage to the destruction of a true free market place economy. My whole effort on trying to help save the USA and western civilization is repealing or getting rid of any wage or price controls entirely, vamooses.

Getting rid of all shackles and restrictions like any wage or price controls is the only way to let loose the miracle working power of a true free market place economy. That way it will have the discipline and power to kick ass and do whatever it may take to save the USA and western civilization.

Otherwise, western civilization might as well start preparing to be on its knees praying five times a day. The fact is western civilization is going to lose this ideology war not in battle but by actually destroying itself. That being said, all the opposing foe needs to do is just walk in and take over.

Right now in the USA alone when this Obamacare insanity collapses the USA economy we are going to be so busy at each others throat, hell, I don't know what to expect. All I can do is pray that I'm not losing my cotton picking mind by letting my imagination get out of control.

Bartender, give me your strongest shot of whiskey, make it a double. There, that should stop any more drift from reality.
INJECTION END.

ECONOMIC INJECTION: SIRMANS LOG: 20 JANUARY 2015, 2108 HOURS.

USA ECONOMY COLLAPSES DUE TO OBAMACARE, MONEY IS WORTHLESS, NO GOVERNMENT CHECKS FORTHCOMING. NOW, IF YOU THINK THAT CAN'T HAPPEN, THEN YOU'RE A FOOL. YOU DON'T KNOW HISTORY; THERE HAS NEVER BEEN A GOVERNMENT THAT DIDN'T FAIL AT SOME POINT.

I CONSIDER IT A CRIME AGAINST HUMAN SURVIVAL FOR ANY GOVERNMENT TO SEDUCE AND MAKE MILLIONS UPON MILLIONS OF PEOPLE SOLELY DEPENDENT ON ANY SYSTEM OTHER THAN THE NUCLEAR AND EXTENDED FAMILY SYSTEM. CREATING A WELFARE STATE IN THE FIRST PLACE IS JUST PLAIN SOCIETAL SUICIDE.
INJECTION END.

I see where the USA and Western Europe leadership are brainstorming and scratching their heads on how to solve the immigration problem, the terrorist problem, the economy problem, etc. Well, as a self-made writer I'm fixing to let her rip. I am not about feel good talk and exercises in futility because in terms of sheer survival winning is everything.

There is no sense of me going back over the destruction of what government as a social and family provider along with the welfare state has done to western civilization. It is very simple "We can't have our cake and eat it too."

I think anyone today with an ounce of economic wisdom should know that western civilization cannot and will not survive as welfare states. And anyone that thinks I'm wrong on this is an educated fool. The old folks used to always say, "An educated fool is the worst kind." I'm warning you, one way or another the days of the welfare state is bankrupt and over.

The sooner the USA and Western Europe realizes that fact the better all of our chances of surviving will be. If you mention "Survival instinct" very few today know what the hell you are talking about. Well, I will tell you what I think it is, the harder the struggle in life the greater it is, the least the struggle in life the least it is.

No one has to tell one with a strong survival instinct that there is no bright future for a civilization with same sex marriages, mass murdering in the womb, and birth control galore. Who is going to produce future generations? Duh! No need for me to nag or preach about morals, today very few give a damn anyway, I'm considered to be the nut case and odd man out.

Moral decay and culture rot in western civilization has become too big and overpowering there simply is no possible way for us to survive as a welfare state. The only thing that can possibly save western civilization is a genuine true free market place economy. But, there is an almost insurmountable problem on acquiring a genuine true free market economy.

It can't be done with any kind of minimum wage or price control law in place. That shackles and prevents a free market economy from disciplining itself which is its greatest strength and asset. The minimum wage law must be repealed or eliminated somehow if western civilization is to survive, period.

Of course I expect no one to heed my great wisdom, power never voluntarily concedes anything, and will always go down with the ship first. So, my favorite cake is chocolate, I'll enjoy my big slice now while I can. Who know what tomorrow may bring.
SIRMANS LOG: 17 JANUARY 2015, 2008 HOURS.

FEDERAL LAW INJECTION: 16 JANUARY 2015, 2111 HOURS.
All of these federal bureaucrats making so-called federal law is non-sense, none of it is real law according to the constitution of the United States of

America.

All we need is a supreme court to come along with the guts and back-bone to announce that from this day forward all federal laws not passed by congress and signed by the president is null and void, period, (Of course pocket veto's and the sort are exceptions).

Case closed. Of course nothing of the sort is ever going to happen, still, the fact is nothing is supposed to be federal law unless passed by congress and signed by the president, period.

The truth shall set you free, and if nothing more, I feel better just saying it. Smile.
INJECTION END.

As a common layman and self-made writer maybe I can explain this separation of powers thing a little clearer. When the founding fathers were setting up our form of government the executive branch of government almost didn't happen.

The first idea was to just have a manager or something of the sort to run the daily operation of government. But, in the end they decided to make it three equal branches of government.

The legislative branch of government would make all laws. The judicial branch of government would interpret and enforce the law according to the USA constitution. And the executive branch of government would carry out the law as written.

However, there seems to be a lot of confusion and misunderstanding concerning presidential executive orders and memos. It really is very simple; the president issuing an executive order is the same as any CEO of a corporation issuing an order or directive to his supervisors and employees.

The president is the commanding chief of the military and head of the executive branch of our government. Eighty or so years ago the president issuing an executive order would mostly affect government agencies and government employees, and had hardly any affect on the vast private sector at all.

That was before the "New deal" when almost no one depended on the government for anything. Well, the hair brained "New Deal" installed act changed all of that. Sure, government must come to the aid of its people but on a temporary basis only.

For government to ever create a permanent class of lifetime dependents is insane. Let's fast forward to today, we live in a welfare state with masses of government social programs and millions upon millions of people solely dependent upon government for survival.

This being the case means any action the government takes is going to affect the private sector almost as much as government agencies and employees.

Still, according to the constitution the separation of government powers is very clear, only the legislative branch of government is entitle to make laws, period.

The executive branch is not entitled to add or take from the law its duty is to carry out the law as written. Don't confuse executive orders with the law. PS: Another problem concerning the separation of powers is far too many judges are legislating from the bench, too, which is especially true with liberal judges.
SIRMANS LOG: 14 JANUARY 2015, 2228 HOURS.

CURRENT EVENTS: GREAT WRITER'S THINKING ON THE 2016 USA PRESIDENTIAL ELECTION WINNER:
I think it will boil down to star power and name recognition versus big money. And providing there is not a total USA economic collapse in 2015 I think in a photo finish star power squeaks out a victory.
SIRMANS LOG: 13 JANUARY 2015, 1336 HOURS.

INJECTION: 10 JANUARY 2015,

1906 HOURS.

Almost everyone think in a free country the government is the most powerful thing, but, that is not necessarily true. I believe ultimately in a free country the economy trumps all. Sure, in terms of raw police and military power the government is all powerful, but, even military power depends on the condition of a nation's economy.

Sure, we are a nation ruled by law, but in the grand scheme of things even the law doesn't have the power of an unshackled and unrestricted free market place economy. What I'm getting at is in a free country ultimately the economy trumps everything.

That is why I keep telling people the evil 1938 socialist minimum wage law de-nuted our economy. That crippled our economy and rendered it weak and helpless to fight off inflation, which our learned economist still calls growth.

That allowed the shallow minded liberals and democrat's to keep superficially expanding our currency enabling them to add social programs and government dependents to no end.

All the while uncle sugar was playing the great super provider daddy role our bread and butter nuclear and extended family units were being destroyed. Uncle sugar was taking away the survival need for a nuclear and extended family unit.

Everything that exists in nature there must be a survival need for it to exist, otherwise it starts ceasing to exist. By uncle sugar taking over as the nuclear family provider, what the hell do you need a nuclear family for, there is no longer a survival need for that, uncle sugar has now taken over that role as the great super provider.

Again, unless our 1938 socialist minimum wage law is eliminated entirely we are a doomed nation in my view, God; I pray that I'm wrong on this.
INJECTION END

For a long time I have believed that an economic collapse would eventually doom western civilization. But, with the ever increasing terrorism around the world I'm not so sure any more. And I will tell you why.

I believe the USA and Western Europe is in denial and unwilling to admit that it is in an all out religious and ideology war. Which, I believe the USA and Western Europe is going to lose unless their minimum wage laws are eliminated entirely.

Western civilization is going to lose this war because of the come about of their socialist welfare state type governments. The come about of the welfare state has made it almost impossible to produce enough men/women of sound judgment and wisdom to protect and safeguard these great nations.

You see, teaching proper norms and traditions to the very young is the only guarantee for maintaining a long term stable and orderly society. We have failed that must do duty, due to our socialist welfare states we have all be destroyed the nuclear and extended family unit which always faithfully carried out this task since the dawn of history.

Uncle Sugar never made sure the very young was raised properly with the love and discipline to be a productive law abiding citizen, that is a must duty of a good provider. A good leader should know that human nature is based on self-interest, logic, and taking the course of least resistance.

That being the case it present the USA and Western Europe with a dilemma that is almost impossible to solve dealing with spending cuts. I'm here to tell you any political party that tries to put a welfare state on a diet is going to run the risk of being chewed up and spit out of power.

In fact the USA and Western Europe I'm afraid has created monster socialist welfare state beast's that's going to set modern civilization back to the Stone Age. Another thing western civilization doesn't seem to grasp is the power of repetition in controlling the minds of people.

An example, some religions has mandatory prayers or chants, mandatory repetition locks in a system and it won't change for ten thousand years. That is what western civilization ideology-wise is up against, and unless the USA and Western Europe can find a way to eliminate their minimum wage laws there is not a snowball chance in hell of winning this battle.

The first hurdle is 98 percent of the general public think having a minimum wage law is a good thing. But, anyone with an ounce of economic wisdom will know that the power of a free market place economy is in its discipline, and any wage or price control prevents it from disciplining itself.

Today's USA economy is like a fast runaway train on a suicide mission to hell barreling its way down the tracks with no way to stop or slow it down. This great writer with almost supernatural wisdom is jumping up and down screaming and hollering that the minimum wage engine governor must have malfunction causing the train to speed up and burn out the brakes.

For God sake smash and get rid of the minimum wage engine governor and the trains accelerator will automatic drop back to zero. And in the future stay away from any minimum wage engine governors

Plus, in the USA almost 50 percent of the people will vote for Santa Claus if he promise to keep the checks coming. They feel what the hell does government paying its bills has to do with voting, take the national debt to 50 trillion, what the hell do I care, duh.

I will say this, in terms of raw human survival there is nothing on earth more powerful than an unshackled and unrestricted free market place economy. Take the minimum wage law shackle chains off and then a genuine true free market place economy will win this ideology and religious war. And save western civilization in the process. Nothing else on earth can do it.

Western civilization is suffering from culture rot and moral decay and has become soft and gullible from years of its socialist welfare state forms of government.

I'm telling you, if any government expects to avoid an economic collapse or being over-run by terrorism it better become lean and mean, and soon. And the only way that can be accomplished is to eliminate any minimum wage law entirely, period.

That will create a lean and mean kick ass unshackled and unrestricted economy. Otherwise, political speaking nothing is going to change and we will just keep wondering how long this can last.

SIRMANS LOG: 08 JANUARY 2015, 2048 HOURS.

INJECTION #4: MY TAKE ON THIS COSBY THING:
HE PRODUCED THE BEST AFRICAN AMERICAN NUCLEAR FAMILY IMAGE

TO EVER EXIST ON TV, BUT, IT IS
UNDER ATTACK AND IS ABOUT TO BE
SENT TO THE JUNK PILE. AND, WHAT
DO WE HAVE LEFT FOR THE NEXT
GENERATIONS, AN IMAGE OF FAST
WOMEN AND HIP HOP THUGS, NOW,
HOW YOU LIKE ME NOW. HOW CAN
WE LET THIS HAPPEN?

I remember a few years back he spoke
in terms of responsibility and
accountability involving African
Americans. If not for that speech none
of this destructive take-down would be
happening in my view. The liberal
entertainment world extremist long
knives are out and they want his scalp,
bad. They feel he sounded too much
like a conservative, and that's an
unforgivable sin, period.
**SIRMANS LOG: 07 JANUARY 2015,
1009 HOURS.**

**INJECTION #3: 23 DECEMBER
2014, 1230 HOURS.**
A BIG REASON WHY AFRICAN
AMERICANS ARE NOT HELD
ACCOUNTABLE AS A RACE IS BECAUSE
OF LIBERAL PATRONIZING. THEY

TEACH THEIR OWN KIDS RIGHT FROM
WRONG AND HOLD THEM TO VERY
HIGH STANDARDS AND SEND THEM
TO THE BEST OF SCHOOLS.

BUT, AT THE SAME TIME ARE OUT
FRONT TREATING AFRICAN
AMERICANS LIKE THEY ARE AN
INFERIOR RACE THAT CAN'T COPE.
READILY PAMPERING AND MAKING
EXCUSES BECAUSE OF SOMETHING
HAPPENED 200 YEARS AGO WHICH IS
MISPLACED BLAME IN MY VIEW.

I SAY NONE SENSE, POPPYCOCK,
BEFORE THIS LIBERAL INDUCED
WELFARE STATE AFRICAN AMERICANS
GOT NO FAVORS AND EXPECTED
NONE THEY EARNED WHAT THEY GOT
SOMETIMES BEING THREE TIMES
BETTER AT A TASK. DON'T INSULT MY
INTELLIGENCE, AFRICAN AMERICANS
CAN COPE AND OBEY THE LAW AS
WELL AS ASIANS OR ANY RACE.

THERE IS NOTHING COMPLICATED
ABOUT THIS MATTER, IT IS VERY
SIMPLE, AFRICAN AMERICANS ARE
NOT TEACHING THEIR YOUNG PROPER
NORMS AND FAMILY TRADITIONS ON

HOW TO BEHAVE AND ACT CIVILIZED. I REST MY CASE, LET THE JURY DECIDE.

SURE, THERE IS ALWAYS TWO SIDES TO EVERYTHING IN LIFE BUT WHERE YOU AIM YOUR FOCUS IS WHAT TRULY MATTERS. I KNOW THERE WILL ALWAYS BE SOME RACIALISM AS LONG AS WE HAVE DIFFERENT RACES.

THERE WILL ALWAYS BE A FEW OVERLY AGGRESSIVE POLICEMEN AS LONG AS WE HAVE POLICEMEN. IT IS THE FOCUS THAT SETS YOU FREE, WE AS AFRICAN AMERICANS HAVE NOT TOTALLY LEARNED HOW TO FORGIVE AND ACCEPT OURSELVES AND THOSE THAT LOOK LIKE US AS BEING AS GOOD AS ANY RACE UNCONDITIONALLY.

UNTIL WE DO THAT WE WILL BE FOREVER PLACING BLAME EVERYWHERE ELSE BUT WITH THE MAN IN THE MIRROR. IT IS A FACT, TRUST AND RESPECT MUST BE EARNED OTHERWISE YOU REAP WHAT YOU SOW. FOLKS, I'M A WRITER,

THAT IS ALL, I HAVE NO POWER TO CHANGE ANYTHING, YOU BELIEVE AS YOU CHOOSE. I HAVE HAD MY SAY. GOD BLESS.

INJECTION #2: 22 DECEMBER 2014, 1406 HOURS.
CAN THE USA SURVIVE IRRESPONSIBLE LEADERS THAT DOESN'T SUPPORT THE RULE OF LAW AND THOSE THAT ENFORCE THE LAW. THOSE THAT EXCUSE LAW BREAKERS ARE WEAK AND LACK THE DISCIPLINE TO BE GOOD LEADERS IN MY VIEW. THAT DON'T MEAN WE ARE NOT A FORGIVING PEOPLE.

THE USA CAN'T SAVE ITSELF; ONLY REPEALING THE EVIL 1938 SOCIALIST MINIMUM WAGE LAW WILL LET THE USA ECONOMY KICK ASS AND SAVE OUR GREAT NATION. MAN CAN'T DO IT.

THE REAL PROBLEM IS WE THE PEOPLE HAVE LOST THIS GREAT COUNTRY BECAUSE OF SHALLOW MINDED LIBERALS AND LIBERALISM. NOW, THE QUESTION IS HOW DO WE

THE PEOPLE TAKE IT BACK, WE CAN'T, BUT THE ECONOMY CAN. AND THE ECONOMY CAN ONLY DO IT BY BECOMING FREE OF THE SHACKLES OF THE CRUEL EVIL 1938 SOCIALIST MINIMUM WAGE LAW.

SURE, ON THE SURFACE A MINIMUM WAGE LAW SEEMS LIKE A GOOD THING BUT IT IS A DAGGER IN THE HEART OF A FREE MARKET PLACE ECONOMY AND RENDERS IT HELPLESS TO FIGHT OFF INFLATION. ALSO, IT ROTS AWAY THE INNER FABRIC OF A NATION UNTIL IT IS MORALLY BANKRUPT.

EXCEPT, OUR LEARNED ECONOMIST AND EGG HEADS DON'T CALL THE DESTRUCTIVE FLAW IN OUR ECONOMY INFLATION, THEY CALL IT GROWTH WHICH IS THE BIGGEST LIE THAT HAS EVER BEEN TOLD. I'M ONE THAT IS NOT FOOLED FOR A SECOND, "YOU CAN'T FOOL ALL OF THE PEOPLE ALL OF THE TIME."

INJECTION #1: 14 DECEMBER 2014, 1430 HOURS.

Churchill said it best, I'm paraphrasing, "Trying to tax your way out of debt is like standing in a bucket and trying to lift it by the handle."

LIFE IS A BLESSING, NO ONE TRULY KNOWS WHAT TOMORROW MAY BRING, WE ALL DANCE TO THE TUNE OF A DISTANCE DRUMMER
By all reasons I shouldn't be a writer but for some unknown force here I am putting pen to paper. My beloved homeland is in far more trouble than meet the eye of most Americans. We are over $18,000,000,000,000,000,000,000 in debt and it is still growing by leaps and bounds.

We are on a sure course to doom, yet we act like sleep walkers by growing our entitlement welfare state even bigger. Folks, I'm going to do something I don't like to do because I think it is self-serving, share secrets and talk about me and my inner self and beliefs.

Here goes, I may look normal, but I am not and never will be. As long as I can remember I have viewed myself as a mentally handicapped cripple. I hate the lime light, and doing anything out front in public. Sure, a few times I have been compelled to be out front but I will always avoid it at all cost.

I will never take a leadership role out front in public because I suffer from several neurotic symptoms. The first neurotic symptom I experienced was when I was around 5 or 6 years old, it started as a result of being whipped for wetting the bed.

I never took it personal or held it against my dad, he believed I was too lazy to get up which was not that uncommon many, many years ago. Anyway, it saddled me with a helpless neurotic pitiful look type symptom that would take over my brain like an epilepsy seizure right before getting those whippings.

Once the symptom started the pitiful look was not limited to just before getting a whipping the symptom could take over my brain in other situations especially if I was tired or before a large crowd of strangers. Over the years I have stayed out of situations that may trip a take over.

I'm telling it now, but most people that have known me all of my 72 years here on earth never knew this about me. The mind is a very power thing and especially with a young child, a bad trauma imprint can last a life time.

Sure, now I have the courage to face and talk about this condition and it doesn't affect me hardly ever anymore. But, I know it is lurking deep in my brain and can still take it over and render me helpless in certain situations.

No one has to tell me how it feels to be humiliated, ridiculed, laughed at, rejected, and on and on, at some time in my life I have experienced it all. But, above it all I believe the saying is true: That what don't kill you will make you stronger. Plus, I learned at a young age those that can genuine love and forgive cannot be mentally destroyed.

Some has tried to do just that to me for whatever reason is beyond me but I am still standing. You name it, hidden cameras, listening devices, GPS tracking, and on and on, yet I am still standing, even when no stone is left unturned. However, who knows what tomorrow may bring, all I know to do is keep pounding my stress call for the survival of my homeland.

I feel it is my destiny to keep sounding the distress call to repeal the cruel evil 1938 socialist minimum wage law entirely. I know 98 percent of the nation's population disagrees with me on this. But, that doesn't prove me wrong; practically all the nation's entire infrastructure like city water and sewage systems, bridges etc. was built before the 1938 minimum wage law.

Nothing else can save the USA from a total economic collapse in my view. And if that happened the government wouldn't have the money to pay these millions upon millions of people depending solely on the government. And if anybody thinks that can't happen he is a fool.

Getting rid of the 1938 socialist minimum wage law will in a controlled way relieve the government of carrying the awesome debt burden of being a social and family provider. With no minimum wage law the people will be able to depend on themselves for survival, not a government already broke and 18 trillion in debt.

I have fought to survive all of my life and I'm telling you the 1938 minimum wage law must be repealed entirely. And to those that don't want to give up any power, you will not have any power anyway if this entitlement welfare state totally collapses. It's going to collapse, there is no doubt about that, exactly when no one knows, but, it may be much sooner than later.

It's just impossible for any nation to survive long term as a super social and family provider, period. It breaks all of the laws of economics. Churchill said it best, I'm paraphrasing, "Trying to tax your way out of debt is like standing in a bucket and trying to lift it by the handle."

Now, I will say something basically the same in my way: Government as a super social and family provider is like a country eating its young, therefore feeding on itself. Also, it is like eating your seed corn and drinking your priming water which is dumb and stupid.

We have around 81 years of our sinister liberal democrat entitlement welfare state and its cost to the government is increasing at warp speed. This cost and debt burden to any government simply can't be sustained. Besides, this liberal shallow brained power grabbing idea of taking on such a cost in the first place for more than on a temporary basis was insane.

Its not only the cost of such a hair brained idea, its effect has left millions upon millions of people dependent minded with no sense of accountability. It has ripped apart this great nation's culture and whole inner fabric to no end.

It has all but destroyed our once strong nuclear and extended family system that has secured the survival of human kind since the dawn of history. Now, when this welfare state government does go belly up all of the millions upon millions of dependents with no sense of responsibility or accountability have little to no chance of survival.

Its too late now, only repealing the evil 1938 socialist minimum wage law entirely can give this great nation a fighting chance of surviving, period. But, only a miracle can make that happen, if I alone seems to have the wisdom to see the light, so be it. Amen.

SIRMANS LOG: 13 DECEMBER 2014, 1541 HOURS.

SECOND INJECTION: 10 DECEMBER 2014, 0755 HOURS:
I BELIEVE AIRING DIRTY LINEN IN PUBLIC DISPLAYS WEAKNESS, SHALLOW MINDNESS, AND A WEAK SURVIVAL INSTINCT, THERE IS NO

VIRTUE IN THAT, CAN THE USA SURVIVE?

Every country is involved in this dark secret cloak and dagger stuff. The reason we have a republic form of government is because depending on the general public is the same as mob rule, that is why the founding fathers wanted us to depend on those we elect to make responsible decisions.

The first rule in anything secret should be to tell only those that have a need to know. There is no need for the general public to know how the intelligence agency sausage is made, that is what we elect our Supposedly responsible leaders for.

In my view only a nation in an almost complete moral and economic decline would tell something so self-destructive. God, I ask in your name, save America from itself. I swear!!!

I take no side in this matter, my point is this sort of dirty linen should be fought out and dealt with out of the public lime light. Many other country does the same thing and far worse. We are not fooling anyone, other countries knows what we are about.

They know what we are doing by exposing this, it shows weakness and self-serving. A great power and country shouldn't have a need to be loved, which is a weakness. And exposing something like this on the public stage equals a need to be loved like we are so good and holy. Now, being respected is a far different matter.

FIRST INJECTION: 04 DECEMBER 2014, 0845 HOURS.

WE AFRICAN AMERICANS INSTEAD OF ACCEPTING OURSELVES AS A RACE UNCONDITIONALLY, WE STILL SUBCONSCIOUSLY WANT THE WHITE SLAVE MASTER IDENTIFY.

WE STILL HAVE NOT BROKEN THE CHAIN THAT WILL FREE US TO BE INDEPENDENT MINDED THINKERS; A HERD MENTALITY STILL CONTROLS US.

OBEDIENCE OF THE LAW MUST BE THE FIRST PRIORITY, FAILURE TO DO SO LEAVES NO EXCUSE FOR WHATEVER MAY HAPPEN

We all care about our loved ones. But, the only thing that keeps us from behaving like wild animals in the jungle is the law. The law must be above all else and the top priority for the USA to remain a civilized nation.

The law must be respected and obeyed, period. We now have the law flaunted and disrespected in high places, and after years of our liberal entitlement welfare state many have succumbed to raw subjective emotionalism. Whatever happened to the words "No one is above the law," are they still valid?

You may want to be weak and stupid and live by the rules of the jungle with little or no respect for the law then have at it, just don't include me. I believe in "First things first," period. The law is what protects us all, especially the poor and disadvantage.

Part of what's wrong with this

entitlement welfare state now is we have turned into a P.... society with less and less accountability. And it's going to be our downfall, you mark my word. Anyone that succumbs to the weakness of subjective emotionalism is a fool and loser, and is either ignorant or not dealing with a full deck in my view.

If one doesn't love and support unconditional one's own race he is without a true identity and can't really be trusted. It's a fact we African Americans are without a true identity and is searching for love in all of the wrong places. I've heard the chant, black and proud and all of that, but in my view it is just words and lack substance.

We need to believe we as African Americans are as good as any race and need to take pride in behaving and obeying the law as well as any race. If you want to be treated with respect, then act like one deserving respect. I believe we as a race can behave and obey the law as well as any race, and we as a race did too before our liberal

entitlement welfare state came about.
SIRMANS LOG: 04 DECEMBER 2014,
1658 HOURS

**SCROLL DOWN TO READ LATEST
INJECTION:**
WE AFRICAN AMERICANS HAS A
PRIMITIVE HERD MENTALITY WITH
VERY LITTLE FREE INDEPENDENT
ACCOUNTABILITY THINKING AMONG
US
Most African Americans have a bond to
the democrat party like a child to its
mother. And no amount of reasoning
or logic can break that bond unless the
child becomes a free independent
minded thinker. Natures law of "taking
the course of least resistance" dictates
that almost no one is going to become
a free independent accountability
thinker unless forced to.

The herd won't allow free independent
accountability thinking within the herd
itself and even when an individual does
it anyway he is branded a traitor or nut
case. Hell, I love my country the only
home I know and I feel if you are
wrong you deserve to be called out

even if you are a sister, brother, or mother.

I don't believe in pampering anyone, you are responsible for your own actions. To err is human, and forgiveness is the foundation of the Christian religion in my view. I'm one that believes that civilization would never have gotten out of the Dark Age without the Christian religion and its power of forgiveness.

My God, I watch the local news almost everyday and its smash and grab, armed robbery, breaking and interring, muggings, and crime galore. And guess who is doing almost all of this crime? You fill in the blank. Yet, all I hear from white liberals and black liberals is patronizing and misplaced guilt and no accountability what so ever, it's insane.

Before the "New deal" a trip behind the shed or woodpile would always keep the would be future criminals on the straight and narrow good citizen course and out of prison. Since that's not done very much any more the best thing that would do the most good for young future black criminals would be medical supervised flogging.

Four or five hard lick on the ass would do far more good than 5-10 in the pen and it wouldn't cost the tax payers. That would put a stop to this paying to produce a more harden and cunning criminal. But, that will never happen, oh, no, we are too civilized for that, yet, the cancer of crime is splitting this great country into racial camps, duh.

Only one thing can save the great USA now: repeal the cruel evil 1938 socialist minimum wage law, then there will be no government forced wage control. That would get rid of any forced wage control entirely. That is the only way this great nation can be saved from itself, period. Repeal it now tomorrow may be too late.
SIRMANS LOG: 30 NOVEMBER 2014, 2123 HOURS.

INJECTION: 02 DECEMBER 2014, 1232 HOURS.
A huge disadvantage with African

Americans having a herd mentality is it has allows a very few poverty pimps to exploit and keep alive this still-a-victim big, big, big, lie. And as long as we have our liberal induced welfare state I see very little chance of African Americans ever being forced to take responsibility and stand on their own to gain a do-and-think-for -yourself mentality.

Sure, I may be hated for my views now, but there will come a day when I will be loved for my great wisdom and foresight, glory be to God.

Just look at our African American situation, in some neighborhoods there is not a husband to be found for miles. And even if you can find a man living in some of the homes all he is there for is companionship and stud service at her whim. Uncle Sam is the real sugar daddy, a poor man can't compete. Come on y'all give me a break now, instead of all of this rioting we as a race ought to be cleaning up our own house.

We ought to be instilling in our young

discipline and self-respect and respect for other people and their property, too. Shame on us for not knowing how to behave and obey the law like other races does. Other races have eyes; they see who is committing all of these crimes. Reality is reality, don't insult my intelligence.

Sure, we as race are guilty of keeping a child's mentality including a fierce sibling rivalry against those who look like us. That is why African Americans can't advance as a race; we won't readily support each other in business or otherwise unless there is no other good choice. And even our elites will try to get as far away from an all black neighborhood as they can afford.

All other races create different pecking order level surrounding zones in their own race's community, lets face facts, and it takes an independent minded adult to escape childhood sibling rivalry. And the first thing it takes to do that is the ability to forgive all people. Otherwise, un-forgiveness locks one in to that situation, then if one is still hating and un-forgiving seventy years later they will still have that fierce dependent minded sibling rivalry from childhood.

To escape here is a simple formula to repeat to yourself over and over until you mean it: "I can wish all people goodwill (through God who strengthens me), optional if you are a Christian." That will free one to become an independent thinker.

I never intended to get sidetracked off into all of this theory stuff, it seems as if my pen took on a life of its own, sorry. Sure, we as a race have some guilt in my view, but again the real arch villain behind the scene is the heavy hand of our liberal induced welfare state beast pulling the strings.

However, before the new deal African Americans had almost thrown off their dependency minded slave mentality, but the welfare state nipped all of that in the bud. Before the new deal blacks supported each other, and we had poor, middle class, and upper class zones in the same community. Plus, we had far more black owned businesses than today. Every town had a booming chitlin's circuit and great entertainment.

We were about to become of age. But, the New deal kicked the poor black man out of the house. After that no one instilled discipline, proper norms, and traditions in our young and we lost our way. After all of that our dependency minded slave mentality returned with a vengeance and the democrat party and the welfare state is now our new slave masters.
SIRMANS LOG: 02 DECEMBER 2014, 1232 HOURS

FERGUSON IS A WAKE-UP CALL ON WHAT CULTURE ROT AND MORAL DECAY HAS DONE TO THE USA DUE TO OUR LIBERAL INDUCED WELFARE STATE.

NEW INJECTION #2, 25 NOVEMBER 2014, 1907 HOURS.
What we African Americans need to realize is each of us is an ambassador

for our race. Many years ago we blacks knew that, but that seems to be lost now a days. A good or bad stereotype image affects all of us in some way, you can't escape it.

Call it what you may but there is no denying the fact that African Americans are committing far more crimes than any race on earth proportional-wise. The main reason for that is lack of parents instilling self-restraint and self-accountability in their young. A lack of self-restraint and self-accountability breeds disrespect for authority and the rights of others.

That is what's driving this out of control cancer in the African American community call crime. But, the actual real villain driving everything from behind the curtain is our liberal induced welfare state beast, with the ability to throw a rock and hide its hand. I stand by my prediction that the USA economy will collapse in 2015 unless our cruel evil 1938 socialist minimum wage law is repealed.

I see all of the economically ignorant do-gooders believing that raising the minimum wage will help people, but, in reality it will only speed up our pace to an economy collapsing doom. Getting rid of any wage or price control entirely is our only way out, because that will restore power back to the people then the people will need very little money and live off the land if need to.

However, there has never been a case of government changing course knowing it is headed to doom, it is not in its DNA. The powers that be is going to feed this tax hungry gobbling welfare state beast to the last crumb.

They will never stop feeding the beast and I will never stop drum beating to repeal our evil 1938 socialist minimum wage law to save the only home and way of life I know. Glory be to God.

SIRMANS LOG: 25 NOVEMBER 2014, 1907 HOURS.

NEW INJECTION: 24 NOVEMBER 2014, 0853 HOURS.

Never in the history of mankind has the poor ever been liberal and moral corrupted until the "New deal" programs created a baby welfare state around 81 years ago. Now we have more poor killing babies in the womb and neutralizing their seed in other ways than any demographic group. No hardship or struggle breeds liberalism and a weak survival instinct.

Anyone with a strong survival instinct (like me) will instinctly know the unborn must be protected for the long term survival of the species. The fact is the USA simply cannot and will not survive unless the cruel evil 1938 socialist minimum wage law is repealed. Any and all types of wage or price controls must be removed entirely.

That will set the all powerful free market place free to save the USA and western civilization, too. Look at the immigration problem in the USA and around the world, its going to engulf us, there is no human solution.

However, if the USA free market was set free by repealing the evil 1938 socialist minimum wage law, then a genuine true free market place armed with nature's supreme law of natural selection would solve the problem and save the USA and western civilization, too.

SIRMANS LOG: 24 NOVEMBER 2014, 0853 HOURS.

PS: I believe they are really fixing to financially knife and gut our beloved military like never before.

WE AFRICAN AMERICANS ARE NOW TREATED LIKE A BUCK

TOOTH REDHEADED STEP CHILD BY THE DEMS.

Political speaking African Americans are now the redheaded step child of the Democrat party. This child has a dependency slave mentality and is totally loyal to his/her care taker. Yet, this child's dependency and loyalty is taken for granted. And now a new adoptee is being favored and groomed ahead of this child, sad, sad.

This child loves and wants to be just like his care taker in every way. This dependent child sees the complexion of his care taker and feels that represents the ideal way one need to be.

However, when the child looks in the mirror he doesn't look like his care taker physically but mentally wants to be as much like his care taker as possible. Plus, this dependent child sees others that look like him as competitors, or even the enemy in winning the most favorite one's role by his care taker. That is why African Americans won't readily support each other in businesses or otherwise if there is a choice. And the beat continues on, as long as this child retains his slave dependency mentality he will not escape his predicament, ever.

The only way out and for this child to acquire free objective independent thinking is to shed his dependent slave mentality. That is a lot easier said than done. It is much easier to follow the herd than to veer off into the unknown and entirely fend for yourself. Also, to take that giant step it is almost impossible when there is a welfare state promising to take care of all in need from cradle to grave.

To take the course of least resistance is embedded in us all. The only thing that is going to get African Americans to be free thinker and independent minded is for the crutch to be kicked from under us. To hell with the victimized mentality, its time African Americans take responsibility individually and as a race and feel responsible for their own survival.

Its time we pull up our pants and face down bad behavior, we know right from wrong, enough of this kindergarten blame, blame, blame game. This cancer crime is out of control in our race and we act like its someone else's problem. There was a time when we blacks had self-respect and behaved as well as any race of people. Why should the Dems treat us with respect, they will continually throwing us a bone every now and then and keep treating us like a buck tooth redheaded step child.

If not for this sinister welfare state African Americans would have long ago shed our dependency slave mentality and still have mostly two parent families.

SIRMANS LOG: 22 NOVEMBER 2014, 1406 HOURS.

MOB RULE, MOB RULE, MOB RULE!!!

Mob rule the very thing the founding fathers feared the most has now come to past. Political polling is just a fancy name for mob rule. We now have out of control do-good emotionalism, while economic ignorance abounds. The law is now treated like an ass.

Folks, we have now arrived. Lord I ask in your name, have mercy on our ignorant souls. And the really sad part is the USA is still the economic engine of the world global economy. And, if the USA economy collapses the world global economy will bite the dust, too. That is all she wrote.

Folks, nothing I say is written in stone, but, mark my words the USA economy will collapse in the year of our Lord

2015. It's too late, nothing can stop it, the stars are aligned and the bust cycle must complete its rotation to make room for the next boom cycle.

Nothing, not even repealing the cruel evil 1938 socialist minimum wage law entirely can stop the collapse. However, repealing the evil 1938 socialist minimum wage law entirely is the only thing that will allow the USA and western civilization to live through this coming collapsing doom.

Otherwise, modern industrial civilization regresses back to the Stone Age. Nature's die has been cast. Dismiss my great supernatural wisdom if you may, we'll soon see.
SIRMANS LOG: 21 NOVEMBER 2014, 1032 HOURS.

SOME PLAIN HONEST POLITICAL TALK BY GREAT WRITER FREDDIE L SIRMANS SR.

Folks, I just felt like doing some plain honest political talk on the status and future the USA. I guess everyone knows that talk radio is dominated by so called conservatives. And let me say up front that at heart I consider myself a conservative, but above all I am a realist.

Sure, I must admit that I am somewhat bias in favor of the conservative view, but to me political extremism is dangerous and counterproductive from the right the same as from the left. I think there is a world of difference between the conservatives of today and the conservatives of the founding father's day.

I think the conservatives in their day had far more wisdom than exist today. In fact in their day almost everyone was conservative. Back then just day to day living demanded one be a conservative if one wanted to survive.

Nature and the elements were harsh and unforgiving which left little opportunity for liberalism to breed.

An easy life and something for nothing is what is necessary for liberalism to breed. Before our "New deal" liberal created welfare state conservatives were men of great wisdom and depth with super strong survive instincts, not these shallow minded liberal like P . . . . . . that abounds today.

Many of the founding fathers were born in Europe and had seen first hand what an all powerful government would do. Now, let's fast forward to today's conservatives. Most of the conservatives of today are just as shallow minded as the liberals, and with weak survival instincts, too.

I will keep it simple; there is no way to instill the necessary proper character in human beings without at least a minimum amount of hardship and struggle, period. Human being has evolved over millions of years and survived aided with an instinct to survive. So, as a rule the harder the struggle and hardship the stronger the instinct to survive. The least amount of hardship and struggle the weaker ones survival instinct will be.

No one acquires the almost supernatural survival instinct I have without some type of great hardship and struggle, mine has been an internal mental battle almost all of my life against self-shame, self-guilt, and things of the sort. However, there is always an exception to everything in life.

The same goes for hardship and struggle, it will make most human beings a better person or even a saint, but a few will become the bitterest one can become. Our liberal induced welfare state has almost completely destroyed our once strong culture and nuclear family system. No one has to tell me this welfare state is over; by instinct I just know it.

I also just know that the social and family provider role must be returned to the people if this great nation is to survive. I also know that our welfare state beast and the powers that be will never voluntarily surrender the social and family provider role back to the people.

That is the reason for my all out assault on the cruel evil 1938 socialist minimum wage law, its repeal is the only vehicle that can wrest the social and family provider role from the government back to the people, and save this great nation from total ruins. I didn't expect the shallow minded liberals to have the depth or wisdom to understand my writing, but I have found that today's conservatives fare little better.

SIRMANS LOG: 18 NOVEMBER

2014, 0038 HOURS

MEMO #2: OBAMACARE WILL COLLAPSE USA ECONOMY IN 2015.

You can't turn back the test of time, the horse has left the barn, the ship has sailed, the train has left the station, you can't put the tooth paste back in the tube, the fat lady has sung, the s... has hit the fan; the cat is out of the bag, the chickens has flew the coop, a day late and a dollar short, and no sense in crying over spilt milk. Those are some metaphors concerning Obamacare.

I predict Obamacare is the straw that is going to break the camels back in 2015, meaning the USA economy. It is going to destroy the best medical system to ever exist. The die has been cast and there is no undoing the damage.

The profit from the USA government survival host (USA businesses) simply can't support its parasite financial load any longer, the load is simply just too great, the economy will collapse in

2015. But, there is a glimmer of hope to keep from losing it all.

The cruel evil 1938 socialist minimum wage law must be repealed to prevent a total collapse all the way back to the Stone Age. And I pray to God that I am totally wrong on this.
UPDATE:
Ever since the "New deal" politicians to buy votes has added layer upon layer of taxes and fees to the cost of doing business. Its over folks, this welfare state beast is not going to tolerate going on a diet. There could be mass civil unrest in 2015 unless the cruel evil 1938 socialist minimum wage law is repealed.

Repealing that evil 1938 socialist minimum wage law will relieve the awesome heavy financial burden load of government being a social and family provider. With no minimum wage law the people will be able to afford providing for themselves.

The economy will then be free with no limit to growth, but, on the other hand it may be possible to buy a week worth of grocery for $5.00. Freedom baby, that's what I'm talking about, being able to eat and survive baby.

SIRMANS LOG: 11 NOVEMBER 2014, 1703 HOURS.

AHOY, AHOY, SHIP AHOY AND FAREWELL TO OUR WELFARE STATE!

Folks, I'm a writer and I know much of my writing seem far fetched, so, accept it as food for thought. OK, let all of the pundits have their say, but you know what they say about opinions, they are like x we all have one. I give my congratulation to the republicans for their great landslide win. Now, you have become like a co-captain to this vastly overloaded slowly sinking welfare state ship.

You have a very, very serious dilemma; this ship is sinking and has very important and needed cargo on board. Much of the cargo is needed for maintenance to keep the ship afloat. To just start cutting and slashing and throwing things overboard may be counterproductive, but the overloaded sinking of the ship must be stopped, and now.

The republicans don't know what to do, nether does the pundits. Enough on the sinking ship analogy; lets get down to some brass tacks. With my supernatural wisdom I believe nothing can stop the USA economy from collapsing, except repealing the evil 1938 socialist minimum wage law, period.

I believe the republican are going to start cutting social programs and that would be the worst course to take at this stage. It will make the economy worse and cause even more frustration. In fact it may be a good thing the republicans doesn't control the presidency at this time. That is because overall the establishment republicans thinking are just as faulty as the liberals and Dems.

Just like the dems and almost all of the USA population think our welfare state can be saved, wrong, it's far too late for that. The republicans think they can fine tune our welfare state beast by doing a little cutting here and there and stimulating the economy to get jobs popping, wrong. This monster welfare state beast is going to chew the republicans up and spit them out.

You just watch, in the next two years I just don't believe anything is going to improve. Of course, I hope I'm wrong on this. I'm sure the only thing that is going to prevent the USA economy from a total collapse in 2015 is to repeal the 1938 minimum wage law. You see humans are motivated and controlled by self-interest. Man can't control nature. Nature's supreme law of natural selection is what actually controls an economy.

Sure, mans actions can greatly influence the economy, but sooner or later every economy is going to complete a boom and bust cycle whether man likes it or not. Man can't stop a long over due bust cycle that is the result of our minimum wage law. But, if the USA untie and free the economy of this insane wage law it will allow us to live through the cycle without a total collapse back to the Stone Age.

The root problem with the USA economy is the liberals has crippled and tied it up by enacting this cruel evil 1938 socialist minimum wage law. That weakens the USA economy where it has no power to fight off inflation or discipline itself. Nothing is going to save the USA economy until it is set free. Otherwise nothing can stop our economy from collapse in 2015.

So, nothing the republicans can do that will truly make much difference unless they free and unbind the USA economy by repealing the 1938 minimum wage law. The establishment republicans like the Dems will try to keep our welfare state beast fed but will fail. And my guess is the liberals and Dems will come roaring back in 2016 with a vengeance and the republicans will be booted out.

One way or another welfare states as super family providers is over and the sooner the USA and western civilization faces that fact the better off we all will be. The first liberal mistake was making the government take on the financial burdens of becoming a permanent social and family provider, because once dependency takes root it is virtually impossible to uproot it.

So, if man can't undo this mistake then free the economy to do the job. Repealing the 1938 socialist minimum wage law will kill two birds with one stone. It will allow the economy to cut off the money supply to our destructive false daddy provider role, and second free the USA economy to kick ass and do what it takes to save our great nation.

A true untied free market place economy with unhindered competition has never in history failed to produce an over abundance of everything a nation need (Jobs).
SIRMANS LOG: 05 NOVEMBER 2014, 1839 HOURS.

POLITICAL POLLING DEFEATS THE PURPOSE OF HAVING A REPUBLIC FORM OF GOVERNMENT.
I know it's not going to happen, but political polling should be banned at least three months before every major political election.

The reason is it defeats the purpose of

having a republic form of government in the first place. The founding fathers to a man all agreed that a republic form of government was best because pure democracy was nothing more than mob rule.

It is true today as it was well over 200 years ago that the general public as a rule is uninformed, emotional, and has a herd instinct. But, one thing the founding fathers didn't know and had no conception of was scientific polling. Instead of the general public voting directly on major decisions governing the country a republic would choose leaders to make those decisions.

The chosen leaders would be elected on what they individually believed and campaigned on, period. That way important decisions governing the country would be insulated from unsound emotional mob rule. That worked just fine until scientific polling came along.

Political polling in my view is nothing more than a fancy name for mob rule. And right now out right mob rule is in total control political-wise. This has allowed the shallow minded irresponsible liberals to exploit the negative emotional weaknesses in our human makeup, which has all but destroyed this great nation.

They have given away the store and promised everyone pie in the sky from cradle to grave. It is the biggest lie that has ever been told. Government must never, and I mean never take on more than a temporary family provider role if any nation is to survive.

It may take as much as eighty years or more, but the destruction die will have been cast. The financial burdens of the family provide role just becomes too heavy for any government to carry. Plus, no nation can survive very long without a strong nuclear and extended family system, which government as a family provider will totally destroy.

Nature's supreme law of natural selection is based on a survival need. Anything in nature without a survival need starts ceasing to exist. Government as family provider takes away the survival need for the private sector nuclear and extended family system until it ceases to exist.

There never has and never will be a society that last over 80-100 years without a strong nuclear and extended family system. It's just not possible because the most critical thing in having a stable long lasting society is instilling proper norms and traditions in the young. And that can't be done without a strong male disciplinarian as head of household, case close. Of course there is always an exception to everything in life.

Government playing daddy just don't

cut the mustard. The USA economy will collapse in 2015 unless the evil 1938 socialist minimum wage law is repealed. If you think I'm crazy and don't know what I'm talking about, your wait won't be very long, we'll see before 2015 is over. And if I'm wrong I'll gladly eat crow.

SIRMANS LOG: 02 NOVEMBER 2014, 1209 HOURS

CAT-CALLS AND WOLF WHISTLING GONE TO THE EXTREME!

I saw the video on TV of the woman that walked three blocks in the Big Apple. And I must admit that I was a little taken aback by the amount of cat calls and wolf whistling that took place. Sure, cat calls and wolf whistling has always been around especially with men in Europe. But, never like what seem to be taking place in the USA today.

The reason I decided to weigh in on

this is because it is a reflection of the moral decay and culture rot that is destroying this great nation. It is the result of our liberal induced welfare state. Government seizing the burden of the social and family provider role for itself and enacting the 1938 minimum wage law, that has ripped the moral fabric of the USA to threads. And the really sad part is very few seem to have the survival instinct or wisdom to give a damn.

There is more to this extreme amount of cat calling and wolf whistling than meet the eye in my view. Before our welfare state this type of behavior was mostly limited to a very very few aggressive males or groups of males. Construction crews have long been known for this type behavior but never over doing it.

Groups of males like to do this sort of thing I believe to make some kind of kinky macho statement, and to impress other males if anything. But, I'm going to give you the real skinny on what I believe has happen to the minds of a lot of men today. Sure, due to our welfare state the USA culture and morals are shot all to hell, but, porn is slowly nailing the lid shut on our coffin.

I believe due to porn a lot of men just don't have respect for women like in the days of old. And I think this extreme amount of cat calling and wolf whistling has an element of contempt and disrespect if more so than admiration.

SIRMANS LOG: 30 OCTOBER 2014, 1953 HOURS.

Government carrying the load burden of social and family provider must end, now. This republic must end this ignorant shallow minded liberal lifetime load burden placed on our government with good intentions. "The road to hell is paved with good intentions."

Sure, after the nuclear and extended family, churches, and social organizations, and as a last resort on a temporary basis government aid is a must. But, to take on permanently a burden that has been with the private sector for over 6,000 years to me is just plain economic ignorance.

Every penny the government survives on comes from the private sector and every dependent the government adds on is one less private sector tax payer, duh. Doing that means it is only a matter of time before the well dries up. That is where the USA and western civilization stands today.

Everyone standing around waiting on big government to provide for them from cradle to grave is a very, very dangerous thing in my view. The bigger government grows the smaller its provider private sector host dwindles until the whole thing collapses. That is what's fixing to happen to this P . . . . of an economy the USA have today.

The only thing that can and will save the USA economy is to repeal the evil cruel 1938 socialist minimum wage law. Any wage or price control is socialist and it ties up and cripples a free market place where it can't purge out inflation, waste, moral decay, and inefficiency.

All that is necessary to save the USA is to repeal the minimum wage law and set the free market free. Then just be still, the free market will take it from there. There is nothing on earth economically wise more powerful than a true unrestricted free market place economy with unlimited competition.

With no plus or minus wage or price controls the free market place will save the USA and western civilization. However, it won't be pretty because a lot of waste, moral decay and inefficiency must be purged in the process. That is the choice the USA faces; otherwise, to stay on course and do nothing means a sure collapse and doom.

Who knows after that, it may mean all the way back to the Stone Age? A true unrestricted free market place economy with unlimited competition has never in the history of mankind failed to produce far more jobs and everything than a nation need. **SIRMANS LOG: 16 OCTOBER 2014, 1149 HOURS.**

WHY I THINK THE USA HAS A P . . . . (PHONY) OF AN ECONOMY.

The downfall and coming doom of the USA can all be traced to the economy. Sure, we are a nation ruled by law instead of men, but, contrary to what almost everyone thinks the economy is the ultimate ruler in a free country.

Authoritarian countries can rule with
an iron fist and demand people toe the
party line or else. But, in free nations
people have the freedom to disagree,
disobey, and to a large degree do as
they please. So, law or no law the real
disciplinarian that truly protects and
safeguards the culture, morals, and
spirituals values in free nations are the
economy.

We in the USA have a weak P . . . . of
an economy that can't even protect
itself from inflation let alone protect
the nation's culture, morals or
anything else. Right now, in the USA
we have strong laws on the book to
stop illegal immigration, crime, and
every vice you can think of, yet, damn
near everything is out of control. This
could never happen with an economy
with any teeth or bite.

All you have to do is look back before
our liberal induce welfare state and

nothing was out of control, which ought to tell you something. The most important thing in maintaining a civil and orderly society is the proper raising of the young, with a balance of love and discipline. In a free nation the economy must be free and untied to maintain discipline.

Economic discipline is what safeguards and protects a nation's culture, morals, and everything else. With a true free market place economy things like the boom and bust cycle and even depressions occasionally are normal. To keep life fit to live nature must have ways to get rid of waste, moral decay, and inefficiency.

Otherwise, there can be no rebirth or re-growth. Then it may be all the way back to the Stone Age the way we are headed. It is even possible for man to disappear from the globe. I could go on and on, on how important a true free market place economy is to the survival of any free nation, but I will start closing this down.

We must untie and free our economy from what the shallow minded liberals did to it by enacting this evil 1938 socialist minimum wage law. What that evil law did was take the strength and power to fight off inflation away from the USA economy. And even today the USA economy doesn't have the power or strength to fight off inflation, let alone protect the nation's culture and morals.

The economy the USA has today is an almost useless, weak, p . . . . of an economy, not a strong kick-ass disciplinarian job producing machine that produced the roaring twenties. Only repealing the evil 1938 socialist minimum wage law can save this great nation. I can only pray that wise men/women will do their duty to save our beloved country.

My extremely wise supernatural wisdom is as threatening to the republican establishment as it is to the liberals and Dem's in my view. You can love me or hate me, but my only concern is the survival of my country. And I'm one that still truly believes in duty, honor, country above all else. **SIRMANS LOG: 02 OCTOBER 2014, 1543 HOURS.**

GREAT WRITER FREDDIE L SIRMANS SR GIVES THE ROCK-HARD COLD-STEEL TRUTH ON DOMESTIC ABUSE.
All I hear is abuse, abuse, wife abuse, child abuse, women abuse and on and on to no end. Liberal women are almost up in arms; and if it was left up to them they would de-nut all men and make sissies out of all of us. To me there is no mystery here, men are just being men, and it is just cause and effect in action in my view. Men are aggressive creatures by nature and are only doing what they are allowed to get away with. And it is a pipe dream to expect law enforcement to do more

than put a dent in it.

It takes fighting fire with fire to really stamp out or completely get under control domestic type violence of this sort. It takes a lot of loved ones that are willing to make a personal sacrifice to truly stamp out or control domestic violence. There has always been some domestic abuse but never out of control like what we are seeing today.

What we are seeing today is the result of a lack of the strong nuclear and extended family unit. Today we have too few no-none-sense kick-ass dads or brothers that are prepared to go to hell or prison before they will tolerate this sort of abuse on a love one. We are too busy using the "N" word on each other to give a damn. Very few cousins or good friends are prepared to make such a sacrifice.

I have personally heard a few men say that the only thing keeping me off her ass is her dad would kill me. Sure, law enforcement will do their job and enforce the law, but no law enforcement agency can protect

private citizens 24-7 day in and day out. Even if women are the weaker sex old man colt solved that imbalance many, many years ago by creating an equalizer. But, the thing about that is not all of us have the will or the guts to send a S.O.B. to hell.
SIRMANS LOG: 19 SEPTEMBER 2014, 2216 HOURS

It really is a waste of time trying to get a liberal to understand freedom and a free market place. That is why most of the world is poor and will always be poor. The point I'm making is liberals don't really understand freedom. Freedom means every individual has a free choice. Jobs don't just drop out of heaven, someone just like you and I must create or provide a job.

This is the land of the free and no one puts a gun to anyone's head and forces them to work for minimum wages. Everyone in this great country has the right to create his/her own job or quit any job one doesn't like. Most liberals think it is wrong for some people to enjoy the rich life while most stay poor. Right now if the liberals had the power they would take almost everything from the rich and spend it on social programs.

They are too shallow minded to realize that rich people are not stupid. They really believe rich people would continue producing and providing jobs while almost all of their earnings are being taken away. I just can't understand how anyone with any common sense could be so shallow, but they are, and are running the country, too.

There never has and never will be a rich and wealthy nation without a lot of rich greedy people to make it happen. If left entirely up to the liberals the USA would in no time be a third world nation. Yet, enough wanting something for nothing voters keep the tax and spend liberals in power while the country goes to hell in a hand basket. **SIRMANS LOG: 12 JANUARY 2014, 2341 HOURS**

A HALF OF A LOAF IS BETTER THAN NOTHING!

IF YOU THINK IT'S GETTING BAD NOW
WITH OBAMACARE, YOU HAVEN'T
SEEN NOTHING YET, YOU JUST WAIT,
IF THE DEM'S WIN ANYTHING IN NOV.
2014, THEN WE WILL GET THE FULL
THROBBING PURPLE SHAFT FROM THE
DEMOCRATS. THEY WANT TO FIRST
SECURE THE 2014 MIDTERM ELECTION
BEFORE THEY RAM THE FULL SHAFT
TO US. IT WILL BE EVEN LESS JOBS
AND A TRILLION MORE IN DEBT. IT
WILL BE LIKE DETROIT CITY
NATIONWIDE! THINK ABOUT IT, WE
WILL THEN GET ALL OF OBAMACARE,
AND DRY, TOO. GOD, I ASK IN YOUR
NAME SAVE THIS GREAT NATION.

It doesn't bother me a lot when I don't
sell a lot of books. That is because I
estimate only around 2 percent of the
American population has the depth and
wisdom to truly understand what the
hell I be talking about. So be it, I carry
on.

They can't get pass the fact that it is

not the amount of money that truly matters; it is the buying power that really counts. Before the New deal which started the welfare state $5.00 would buy more than $50.00 will today.

Repealing the minimum wage law would put the provider role back into the hands of the people and allow this great country to survive. Otherwise, there is no way in hell the USA is going to survive on its present course.

Just keep on believing in this phony minimum wage economy and without a doubt within a year I will be proven right. We'll soon see just how nutty my predictions are.

The repeal of the minimum wage law is our savior, but, 98 percent of the population can't get pass believing more and bigger is always better. But, to me a half of a loaf is better than nothing because nothing is what this

nation is going to get if we don't change course.
SIRMANS LOG: 29 DECEMBER 2013, 1022 HOURS.

MAN/WOMAN OVERBOARD, USA ECONOMY SHIP IS BEGINNING TO SINK!
Folks, I'm just a lowly unknown writer out here pounding away trying to get through to thick sculls. Very few actually know about me or my books, and most of those that do are not interesting in tough accountability and responsibility. But, I know without a doubt at some point my writing will be vindicated.

Reality is reality there is just no way of getting around that fact. Sure, sometimes it takes a while for the results to catch up but there are no free rides in life someone always pays. The liberals and Dem's have been very successful; they have created masses upon masses of government dependents. They have convinced these dependents that government will always be there to take care of them and their needs.

That is not reality that is the biggest lie that has ever been told. There has never been a government that didn't go broke at some point. The free market place made the USA the most richest and powerful nation to ever exist. The government didn't do that, the free market place did that. Now, I believe most of the people running our government today doesn't even believe in a free market place.

I believe most of the people in charge of our government today are socialist or communist at heart. Everyone seems to be so surprised about how the liberals and Dem's connived and forced Obamacare down our throats. There is nothing new here about liberals in my view. How in the hell do

you think the liberals and Dem's held on to the USA house
of Representative for 40 consecutive years.

They did it by lying and conniving, and that is what is really happening with this Obamacare website. They will never let it work right before the November 2014 election. They intend to keep the confusion going and never let all of the high costs be widely known before the 2014 election. But, God help us if the Dem's win anything in November 2014, because if they do they are going to ram the full purple shaft to this free nation, e.g. Obamacare dry like it or not.

I believe these people are hardcore ideologues and will go down with the ship before yielding an inch, and believe me that is exactly what is about to happen. Trust me, this USA economy ship is taking on too big of a load and is beginning to sink. This ship is going down unless most of its government load is jettisoned, and fast.

However, the only way to lighten governments load is to kick it out of its social and family provider role. And the way to do that is repeal the minimum wage law or else, this economy ship is going down. I suspect many of the rats have already left the ship in spirit and have property in in places like New Zealand and Australia.

SIRMANS LOG: 26 DECEMBER 2013, 1840 HOURS

WHO IS THE AFRICAN AMERICAN COMMUNITY'S DADDY?
I'm fixing to briefly weigh in on something I have no business touching, besides, some people think of me as a nut case anyway. What if I am off the beaten path that don't mean my beliefs are wrong. Even a broken clock is right twice a

day. Concerning two great black athletes that is at loggerheads: Long before O. J. got into trouble, guess who was always on his case for being too white? Go figure? Some people just naturally goes against the grain, enough said. The problem with the African American race as a whole is culture.

The welfare state has destroyed the African American family structure and community. But, that don't mean we have to take it lying down and still not feel responsible for our own behavior and survival. I don't have the power to stop anything, but you can bet your bottom dollar that I will never make excuses for bad behavior. And no matter who does it I'm not accepting any excuses because of what happened in the distance past.

Grow up African Americans and take responsibility for the behavior of yourself and that of your race. This welfare state has destroyed accountability and responsibility throughout all of America and I'm sick and tired of it. Today a decent law abiding black man can't walk into many stores without being feared because we as a race won't clean up our own community house.

Don't tell me that ain't from a lack of feeling responsible for our own behavior as individuals and as a race. We still have a dependent slave mentality and think it's the white mans fault. The only cure for that is for someone to kick the crutch from under us and demand we stand on our own two feet. Independent minded people don't look to blame and find excuses to fail. I know I may sounds cold, but this USA economy is fixing to collapse and we black folks need to wake up and be prepared, now.

Every preacher in the pulpit and any member in the black community with an ounce of authority need to feel responsible for this cancer in our community called crime. I don't mean taking any physical action we have law enforcement for that. What I'm talking about is taking a moral stand instead of not feeling racially responsible for bad behavior in our youth.

If we don't save our youths no other race will. I didn't intend to vent like this, I just got carried away but something's need to be said. The so called African American leadership is out to lunch.
SIRMANS LOG: 18 DECEMBER 2013, 1750 HOURS

THERE IS NO GOVERNMENT SYSTEM EVER TO EXIST MORE SELF-DESTRUCTIVE THAN A WELFARE STATE!
Like a junkie on the streets trying to get a fix there is nothing a welfare state won't sell off to support its seized

social and family provider role. As long as the USA government stays in its social and family provider role it will be impossible for the USA to stop reckless spending or survive.

Right now, the liberals doesn't have the survival instinct or the wisdom to see a real need to stop spending. They are living in the moment and can't see any real danger in reckless spending, and you couple that with an economically ignorant main stream press and general public, all I know to do is pray.

Abolishing the minimum wage law will give the social and family provider role back to the people where it belongs and has always been until the "New deal" seized it in 1938. God I ask in your name, "Save the USA." Time is a winding down, I don't know how much we have left, but, I know beyond a shadow of doubt that a total economic collapse is near unless drastic changes are made.

When I look at the future I think the republicans will soon get the power to have their shot at this health care thing. But, I have news for them too, just like the Dem's they think government can keep and hold on to its social and family provider role, wrong.

I believe unless the republicans and conservatives set about abolishing the minimum wage law they will be seen as phony liberals and quickly replaced. But, of course do like the Dem's never admit in advance what your real intentions are, just git in there and rid the country of this Minimum wage law. It's a free market place killer. See Sirmans survival plan further down.

Most of the big cities water, sewage, and bridges infrastructure were built before a minimum wage law, so, don't tell me junking the minimum wage law won't save this great nation. And here is the real kicker: The USA economy is still the economic engine of the world and if it collapses it takes the world economy down with it. Sure, the world economy may bail us, but not before owning us.

The apple cart has been upset and the only thing that can save the USA is a true free market place. Pure communism and socialism never has and never will work, but, now we have a new monster far worse than both of those systems to contend with, it's called the welfare state. There is no system ever to exist more self-destructive than a welfare state.

It leaves almost no survival tools in place to survival on when nature's bust cycle comes around or if the economy collapses. It really is no joke when I say it may be all the way back to the Stone age for modern civilization. We have no strong nuclear and extended family system to survive on. We have centralized factory farming for our meats and vegetables and hardly any small farmers and home gardeners.

That means we have no adequate emergency backup bartering capacity if the economy collapses and money is worthless. And on and on, our family morals and values would make dog eat dog look like a Sunday picnic after a week into a collapse. Wages and prices must be free floating for a genuine free market place to work and that can't happen with a minimum wage law or any kind of wage or price control.

The consumer cost of living is what's going to kill off the USA economy and Obamacare just speeds up the process. Here is the Ultimatum: Either the USA government abolish the minimum wage law which will free the people to save themselves and the country, or it tries to consolidate and hold on to its current social and family provider role.

If it chooses the latter there is no doubt in my mind that it will to no avail sell off the country to foreigners to try to hang on to a role it shouldn't be in, in the first place. You just watch, and the wait won't be very long. I can dissect an economy as well as anyone and that is what I predict is going to happen. You can't get blood out of a turnip.

I doubt there is any gold left at Fort Knox and there is no telling what else has already been sold off by the federal reserve. I'm telling you as a man of great super natural wisdom, unless the minimum wage law is abolished we might as well kiss our freedom and this great country good by forever.

SIRMANS LOG: 04 DECEMBER 2013, 2217 HOURS.

AMERICA! YOU HAVE BEEN SOLD A

FALSE BILL OF GOODS.

There is a sucker born everyday. It amazes me how gullible people are. They have fallen for this cock & bull big lie that the Obamacare website is somehow a big screw-up, wrong. I for one don't buy that for one second. A computer or a website must obey what it is programmed to do.

The problem is: There is no way in the hell liberals and Dem's are going to let it be known on a large scale the double and triple cost the people will face until after November 2014. Get a grip America; you have been sold a false bill of goods. And be prepared for a never ending list of excuses, but, you will never get a proper working website with cost no matter what you are told. I rest my case.

SIRMANS LOG: 30 NOVEMBER 2013, 2216 HOURS.

MAN HAS NEVER SET FOOT ON THE

MOON? SIRMANS LOG: 02 JUNE 2013, 1750 HOURS.

Awhile back I wrote an article that I was 99.9 percent sure that man landed on the moon but I still can't get past that .1 percent. It's not that I am dumb or stupid; I understand electronics and modern science.

Right out of high school back in 1962 I took a six month course in radio and TV repair. Back then we studied mainly the super heterodyne receiver and vacuum tubes. The transistor was just coming into play the same as the cathode ray vacuum tube which was the early TV.

We also learned about waves and frequencies. So, on my part it just doesn't make any sense for me to doubt that they landed on the moon. When I wrote the first article on this subject a guy asked me in a comment did I have any proof that they didn't land on the moon, and I said "No."

In replying I told him it was just a gut feeling, and that is still what haunts me on how I feel about the whole matter. There is something about this whole thing that logical just doesn't add up in my way of thinking. I feel something is wrong somewhere.

Even if they did land, maybe they found something up there (UFO) that they are not telling. I have a fair understanding of human nature, and there have never been a case where man opened up a new frontier and didn't exploit it in some way.

Like I said, maybe there is a big hidden mystery that maybe it's better the public never knows about. I don't have any inside information, just a raw gut feeling. This article may be the smoking gun or the last straw that I really am a nut, kook, or loon, who cares, some already believe that anyway.

However, I am not entirely alone doubting that man landed on the moon, 10 percent of the USA population is Doubting Thomas's on this. God bless America.

PS: I see where they use the terrain in the state of Utah to train for the moon landing. You don't suppose they use that same terrain to make moon landing movies do you? (Just kidding y'all).

THE USA LAST SUPPER!
SIRMANS LOG: 9 JUNE 2013, 1954 HOURS
Anyone that can stomach reading my work knows that I have a super mind agree or not. So, I have decided to draw a picture and explain what happened to the great USA. I think it boils down to two word "Sound judgment."

Starting with me, probably three percent or less of the USA population agree or truly understand my way of thinking. The vast majority think my writing is some kind of nineteenth century throwback. And they are mostly right, a hundred years ago about ninety five percent of the USA population would have agreed with my way of thinking.

Back then same sex marriage and mass killing in the womb would have been beyond everyone's imagination. Now, ninety five percent or more of the USA population see that as normal. The USA is about evenly split down the middle in terms of voting.

The masses of government dependents see the republicans as the enemy and believe they would like to take away their livelihood. The other half believes the democrats are going to tax and spend the USA out of existence. But, I believe like one politician said: "There

is not a dime worth of difference
between the two parties."

Sure, there are minor differences in
terms of appointing judges but neither
party is going to serious stop the
growth of government. Overall the
Dems and liberals are the reason the
USA is in the dire situation it is today.
In my view Dems and liberals are just
plain shallow, but, super aggressive
and will not let morality, country, or
anything stand in the way of them
grabbing and taking power.

On the other hand the Republican
Party has become almost as liberal as
the democrat party. I feel the
conservatives ought to just flat out
take it over. Even conservatives don't
agree with my out dated thinking, still
I think they are the only ones that can
save the USA from total doom.

The thing is they don't know how.
Well, it may already be too late but I

am going to tell them how to save the USA. However, I'm sure they won't agree and won't take my advice; still I'm going to pass it on anyway. Remember, I said the Key words were "Sound judgment." The Dems and liberals own the thinking and shaping of young minds in the USA.

For over 6,000 years up until the "New deal" the nuclear and extended family system was the primary shaper of young minds, but, not anymore. To a great extent in most situations now the primary shaper of young minds is liberal TV and the liberal school systems. Very few homes are instilling traditional conservative's norms and values.

Almost everything the young comes in contact with now-a-days is liberal. So, of course the young when they mature will not have a conservative foundation to return to like children of old. "Sound judgment" which is everything to keep

and maintain a civil society will soon
be nowhere to be found.

So, my advice to conservatives is
follow my advice cold turkey and go for
the jugular. No if ands or buts, fight to
abolish the minimum wage law now,
not tomorrow. With no minimum wage
law the government will lose it power
to control private property.

With no minimum wage law
government would have to give up its
provider role which has all but
destroyed our nuclear and extended
family system. With no minimum wage
law manufacturing would return to the
USA and everything would be made in
America with jobs for all.

With no minimum wage law the
economy would balance itself and the
poor could pay their own food and
medical bills. With no minimum wage
law people would make far less money
but $5.00 would buy A week's worth of

grocery. And I could go on and on what has been proven to work for over 6,000 years before the "New deal."

Plus here are the cold steel facts, if the minimum wage law is not abolished, the USA is not going to survive and that is a guarantee. Before the "New deal" the male nuclear family provider hands on instilled and enforced norms and traditional conservatives values thereby safe guarding our human survival.

Now, unless the government is kicked out of the provider role the USA has the chance of a snowball in hell of surviving. Abolishing the minimum wage will get the ball rolling on saving my beloved homeland.

I believe in a few months when Obamacare fully kicks in it is going to explode the dole and cause the USA economy to crash and burn. I also believe abolishing the minimum wage law is the only way to stop the USA economy from crashing and burning.

Will congress abolish the minimum wage law? NO! Will the USA and western civilization survive? NO! Reason, the boom and bust cycle is a part of nature the same as the life and death cycle.

Abolishing the minimum wage law would have save us by allowing the bust cycle to complete it normal rotation, but no, the learned economist and egg heads think they can juggle the figures forever, wrong.

Call me a fool or nut as you wish, but without a doubt I know I am right on this. Sure, no one agrees with me on any of this but they will, the hardship and suffering just hasn't taken it toll yet.

USA SUPREME COURT CONFIRMS

THE VALIDITY OF MY WRITING!

For over twenty years even I at times have questioned the worth or validity of my writing. But, not anymore, since the supreme court all but struck down the defensive marriage act on 26 JUNE 2013.

Folks, it's over for the great USA and western civilization. And the really sad part is very few people even realize it. It is very simple, there has never been and never will be a civilization that last over 80-100 years without a strong nuclear and extended family system, period.

What the Supreme Court did was drive the final nail in the coffin of a strong nuclear and extended family system. Now! Let me tell you why I know I am right beyond a shadow of a doubt. The nuclear and extended family system has kept civilization intact for over 6,000 years.

That was until the early 1930's in the USA when a group of liberal geniuses did something that had never been done in the history of mankind; they seized the family provider role for the government itself. Wow! Wham! Bam! Armed with the "New deal" programs the government became "The great white father" and sugar daddy.

What the shallow minded liberals failed to realize and still haven't to this day is understand that the provider role is the Key to civilization and its survival. What is taught and instilled in the young is what maintains and keep society stable and intact.

Norms and traditions must be instilled for safety and survival because they are based on past trial and experience. This must duty for over 6,000 years was tasked to the provider of each nuclear family unit. The nuclear family provider is the only one with the power and authority to make sure this must duty is carried out.

The family provider should have the physical, financial, and moral capacity to perform this duty thereby safeguarding and maintaining a healthy civilized society. Well, we all know what happened; the USA government seized the provider role for itself and got drunk on power. So, you can forget about it yielding even one inch, ever.

Sure, it provided food and shelter, but failed to enforce any other must provider duty. Failure by the government as the provider to make sure norms and traditions were instilled in the young meant death to the USA four generations into the future. And sure enough here we are around four generations later with almost everything ass backward.

Same sex marriage and mass killing in the womb seem to be the norm today which would have been insane at the time, and now sound judgment is something you find in the history books. And, you are going to convince me that this nation can survive, @#%$*%$#, I love you too!

But, due to my great supernatural wisdom I see one last chance for the USA to survive. And we can still survive with freedom still intact provided we as a nation abolish the

minimum wage law; otherwise we go the way of the great Auk.
SIRMANS LOG: 27 JUNE 2013, 1255 HOURS.

THE FULL DESTRUCTIVE FORCE OF OBAMACARE IS FIXING TO HIT!

All seems to be calm and quiet on the home front; they say the housing market is booming. So, what is there to fear? It is almost always quiet before the storm. I'll tell you what's lurking out there, the full destructive force of Obamacare is about to hit.

I also predict that the dole is likely to explode and then all hell is going to break lose when Obamacare fully hit. So, my advice is brace yourself the s... is about to hit the fan. There is already a mad rush by businesses to stay below 50 employees and keep the work week below 30 hours.

There is already over 48,000.000 million on the food stamps dole alone, plus, we are already $17,000.000.000.000 trillion in debt and borrowing 40 cents of every dollar the government spends. Now, you are going to convince me otherwise that at some point the USA government is not going to prostitute our sovereignty away?#@%!, spare me.

So, in a few more months when Obamacare fully kicks in it may be Katie bar the door. In my view everything Washington enacts now if it's not to abolish the minimum wage law is going to be an exercise in futility.

I think the USA is at a do or die stage, and dealing with the root problem first is a must and anything else is a waste of precious time. I see the USA destructive root problem as government's seized role of being a "Social and family provider."

The USA government as a social and family provider has ran it course which is a role it should never have gotten into in the first place. The "New deal" seized the provider role from the nuclear and extended family system where it had been for over 6,000 years.

Until the USA government gets the hell out of the social and family provider business the USA cannot and will not survive, period. It's just that simple, either the USA government jettisons its social and family provider role or we go the way of the great auk, there is no way to get around that fact.

The only way to save the USA before a total economic collapse results from Obamacare and an exploding dole is to abolish the minimum wage law now. I know in today's climate very few has the wisdom or depth to see how abolishing the minimum wage would save the USA economy.

That is why I really don't see the minimum wage ever being abolishing voluntarily, still, I must never stop pounding for it. Even if no one else do I know only abolishing the minimum wage can safely bleed off the pressure and save the USA economy, because there is no doubt in my mind it is fixing to blow or collapse.

Sure, before the "New deal" there was

much suffering especially the elderly. But, the tried and true nuclear and extended family provider system has proven itself for over 6,000 years, it's not perfect, but it works and doesn't destroy morality. Plus, the nuclear and extended family provider system is never a threat to bring down the whole system and send us all back to the Stone Age.

Whereas, the "New deal" has given us this tax hungry welfare state socialist beast. This beast has all but destroyed the nuclear family, family values, and sunk our morals to the point that we have same sex marriage and mass killing of the unborn in the womb. And even worse, very few USA citizens even care or give a damn, to them that's just the new norm.

Yet, someone like me is seen as a nut case and a throw back that should be ignored or locked away some where. With all of this going on the USA cannot and will not survive unless the minimum wage is abolished to bring back some sanity.

We are just too far gone into this swamp of value rot and moral decay, only a physical barrier like abolishing the minimum wage can save us now. Man is control by logic and self-interest which means the way to hell is paved with good intentions.

"Be still God will fight your battle," but, in this case, abolish the "Minimum wage law, then be still, and the invisible hand which is nature's supreme law of "Natural selection" will save the USA economy and western civilization, too.
SIRMANS LOG: 9 MAY 2013, 1243 HOURS.

FREDDIE L SIRMANS SR. SHORT BASIC LECTURE ON UNDERSTANDING AN ECONOMY!
Am I dumb, ignorant, or just plain stupid, I'm sure many people think so because I keep harping on abolishing the minimum wage law. What if I am a kook or loon, still, that don't prove me wrong. Sure, when you look at it on an individual or personal basis obviously no one want to make less income.

On the surface a minimum wage seems like a good thing just like most things that have create this welfare state beast we have. In my view even most learned economist doesn't really understand how a free market place economy is supposed to work.

The real truth is it is nature's supreme law of "Natural selection" that really controls everything in nature including the working of an economy. And anyone that doesn't understand nature can never understand an economy.

The first understanding is listening to the words, it says natural selection and free market, force is nowhere to be found. So, that means the first rule to understanding an economy is force will never get you the most production out of an economy.

A minimum wage law is the use of

force and it slows production and may even bring growth to a halt. Without a minimum wage law many more businesses could start small and grow into giants.

Many big business men will tell you that if they had to start today they could never have gotten off the ground. All a minimum wage really does in terms of progress is give more power to the government to control private property.

The minimum wage law keeps money inflated for government to have enough to pay one group not to work and tax the other group to death which allows government to stay drunk on power. Right now the government have taken over and own far more private property than a hundred years ago and will probably end up owning it all.

Another reason why people don't understand economics is first you have to understand human nature to understand economics. A good example is "Greed," almost everyone thinks greed is a bad thing for an economy, wrong; nothing could be further from the truth.

Nothing can replace greed. There is no greater energy packed motivating force in our entire human makeup than greed. Greed is something that must be harnessed, but, never smothered out or severely restricted if you want a successful economy.

There has never been a rich and prosperous nation without a lot of greedy people to make it happen. Greed can be compared to electricity, very dangerous, but very little progress can be made in terms of wealth without it.

A free market place with free

competition is the perfect way to harness greed without smothering or snuffing it out, like the communist or socialist. There never have been and never will be a rich and prosperous pure communist or socialist state.

The USA is no longer even close to having a genuine free market place. A genuine free market economic have never in history failed to produce far more than that nation can use in almost everything.

Yet those in power that love power and control may tolerate the free market but still hate it. The reason power hungry leaders don't like the free market is kin or no kin if you don't produce you are gone.

In closing I will add this little nugget: To create great wealth one must be willing to take great risk. But, no one is going to take great risk without a fair chance for a great reward, period. Why work extra hard and produce more when non producers get an equal share that is where the great USA seems to be headed.

I hope my short economic lecture have been helpful to you in some way. I am a creative self-made writer; most of what you get is my own original thinking.

SIRMANS LOG: 16 MAY 2013, 2056 HOURS.

EXTRA INPUT: 23 MAY 2013, 0135 HOURS.

Let me say this to around 95 percent of the USA population that strongly disagrees with me and my views on abolishing the minimum wage law, there is a very important question that you have failed to ask.

That question is: what are you and the country going to do when the USA government doesn't have the money and can't borrow it to pay its bills. Huh! That's the problem! Over 95 percent of the USA population have never imagined let alone asked a question of the sort.

Almost everyone seems to think of the USA government as some kind of omnipotent money sow that we can suck on her tits forever. But, nothing could be further from the truth. There never has been and never will be a government that doesn't go broke at some point.

Even worse, the USA has a social and family provider government that amounts to a socialist welfare state. The USA economy not only can collapse it will collapse as soon as Obamacare fully kicks in in a few months.

No matter what the learned economist and egg heads may tell you, self-made writer little ole me is telling you the USA economy is on the brink and when Obamacare fully kicks in it will collapse.

Sure, probably no one is going to believe me, no problem, we all will know in a few months if the USA economy can swallow Obamacare and survive.

Of course, any suspense could be avoided if the USA just took the bull by the horns and abolished the minimum wage law which would no doubt save the USA economy.

THE "NEW DEAL" CURSE!
Family discipline is the extremely important ingredient that has been missing in the USA ever since the "New deal" seized the provider role from the nuclear and extended family system.

The nuclear and extended family system is where the provider role stayed for over 6,000 years until the "New deal" seized it in the name of Mr. Do-gooder.

However, being a provider is much, much more than just providing food and shelter. The provider is the only one with the power and control to enforce and maintain discipline and instill it in the young.

For any society to survive over four generations the provider must safeguard norms and traditions and make sure they are instilled in the young.

So, when the shallow minded liberals armed with the "New deal" seized the provider role for itself it failed to take on provider duties and responsibilities that have been carried out for over 6,000 years. And the liberals are still doing this crime against USA society.

This shallow senseless liberal

destruction has devastated and all but destroyed the African American community in the USA and the cancer is well on it's way to destroying all of USA society.

Now, here we are in the year of our Lord two thousand thirteenth year with 95 percent of the USA population left with the survival instinct of a 10 year old.

We are at death door in terms of human survival with all of our eggs in one basket. We solely depend on a bloated wobbly kneed socialist welfare state beast that could totally collapse any moment and send civilization all the way back to the stone age.

No society can survive without a strong nuclear and extended family system, a strong moral and spiritual code in place, and adequate emergency backup bartering capacity with many small farmers and home gardeners.

Those were the survival tools that allowed western civilization to survive the great depression, which today is practically nonexistent. The stone age may be our only destination.

That is because nature's law of "Boom and Bust" is like the life and death cycle there can be no long term survival unless it is carried out. Yet, here I am with an almost super natural strong survival instinct and I'm seen as a nut, kook, loon, or some other reject or hater.

I plead and I plead for sanity like abolishing the minimum wage law which I know will save my beloved homeland, the only home I know.

Having this great wisdom and super strong survival instinct is like a curse to me; I can dissect an economy and see straight to the core of most things when so many just don't get it. God, I ask in your name bless the USA home of the brave and the free.

SLAVE FIELD-HAND MENTALITY GRIP STILL BINDING.

Wake up African American political and spiritual leadership, grow up and take responsibility, you are not a field-hand anymore. You are now up on the hill in the big house now.

You must now take on the responsibility of running the place. You must now create your own jobs and means of making a living. You must set a budget and make sure the family gets fed, whereas as a field-hand all you had to do was work and obey orders.

You are now the master of your own destiny now, if you don't do it yourself it may not get done, you are not a dependent anymore. Fast forward to the year of our Lord 2013, the African

American race has a serious problem.

People are afraid of African American men, especially young black males. Reality is reality and it is what it is. There is an old saying: You can't make other people change, but, you can change yourself then the world around you will change.

If you don't believe that here is an example: Stress: If anyone on your job or anywhere causes you a lot of stress, just repeat this quote to yourself over and over as long as necessary, "I can wish all people goodwill no matter how they treat me," then the stress will vanish. This is only a tool and not for every situation.

Black males are stereotyped as dangerous and violent prone. A stereotype can be overcome and gotten rid of. You get rid of a stereotype by proving over time that it is no longer true. But, that can't be done until one accepts responsibility and stop blaming circumstance and the system.

There is no excuse why Africans Americans can't obey the law and behave as good as any race, period. Any winning coach will tell you, you are going to get some bad calls but you focus even harder on your game plan.

Sure, as a minority the system may not give a black man a break and in some cases may even be unfair, still, there is no excuse why African Americans can't obey the law and behave as good as any Race.

I'm over seventy and from the Deep South and I remember before the welfare state destroyed the black family, no one feared a black man walking into a country store.

Many years ago in the USA the

Japanese were stereotyped as the junk and trinket merchants. But, through hard work and quality control they proved that they could produce as good a product as any nation. Today no one doubts the quality of Japanese products.

African American political and spiritual leaders need to believe and prove that the African American race can behave and obey the law as good as any race, period. Like me or hate me, still, how can any self-respecting responsible African American disagree with me on this, (SMH) shake my head.

The black community itself suffers more than anyone from all of this violence. Do-for-myself responsible hands need to grab the MLK, Jr. baton and take it into the home stretch to full equality and justice.

And, tell the liberals we don't need your pity or patronizing services any

longer
SIRMANS LOG: 27 AUGUSTA 2013, 2135 HOURS.

IS MASS STARVATION AND SUFFERING AHEAD FOR THE USA?
Almost everyone thinks that I'm really the nut and stupid one for constantly wanting to eliminate the minimum wage law entirely.

Well, I know and anyone with a deep understanding of economics knows that the USA and world economy may soon collapse. When this happens the minimum wage law will disappear and there may be chaos, mass suffering, and starvation if we survive at all.

So, all I'm saying is why go through all of that un-necessarily
when voluntarily abolishing the minimum wage law will prevent it. One way or another the minimum wage will go the way of the great Auk, (SMDH)

shake my damn head.

Obamacare is simply the straw that is going to break the camels back.
SIRMANS LOG: 25 AUGUST 2013, 1834 HOURS

"OUR FALSE GOD OF DOOM!"
Just like the big enemy armored divisions of World War II ran on ball bearings our liberal created welfare state runs on the minimum wage law. In sheer economic terms the minimum wage law is "Our false God of doom."

It is impossible to save the USA or western civilization unless the minimum wage law death grip is broken. The laws of economics demands that the minimum wage law must go or the USA bites the dust.
SIRMANS LOG: 24 AUGUST 2013, 0625 HOURS.

YOUNG CHILDHOOD SEXUAL ABUSE!

This doesn't belong here and I shouldn't be saying it anyway, it concerns childhood sexual abuse. My view is very simple; if you do the crime you do the time or pay with your life, period.

The good book says flee from temptation, which a wise man will heed to. Contrary to what most people may think there are abnormal forces out there that are almost impossible to resist unless one flees.

Example: A young child sexually abused may become obsessed with sex and become armed with the power of sexual projection. The child grows up but the abnormal power of projection remains. Now, if someone with this abnormal power focuses it on you for whatever reason, your best bet is to get the hell out of Dodge and fast.

Enough said, something like this is never talked about anyway. Ignorance is bliss and just thank God nothing like this has ever happened to you. Believe it or not there are forces out there that only a strong moral and spiritual person can withstand, it's rare, but, it does exist.

"The human mind is a very powerful thing".
SIRMANS LOG: 20 AUGUST 2013, 1138 HOURS

IS A GOVERNMENT SHUTDOWN INEVITABLE?
Right or wrong the republicans are stupid if they force any issue that will end in a government shut down. It will be a lose, lose situation for republicans any way you look at it.

The liberals including the vast majority of the mass media in my view will have a blaming field day. Besides, after the first huge public outcry the vast majority of the republicans will head for the tall grass or high tail it out of Dodge anyway. And even if the republicans could win some kind of hollow victory, very little would change, we still remain a welfare state.

This welfare state is on automatic pilot and nothing or nobody is going to stop it unless its fuel is cut off. Sure, a collapse will stop it but no sane reasonable person wants that, cutting spending won't stop it that will only get the republicans out of office.

Believe it or not, the fuel that propels this whole welfare state is the minimum wage. It is impossible for the USA to survive as a welfare state. But, it is also impossible for the USA to get out of being a welfare state when government sets any wage or price control.

You can't have a true free market economy when government sets any amount of wage or price control. The minimum wage law allows government to inflate the currency so it can keep its power as a super social and family provider.

But, government should never be a social and family provider in the first place because that destroys the nuclear and extended family system. Without a strong nuclear family system it is impossible to remain a free people after four generations.

If the republicans really want to go to the mat for something do something sane like abolishing the minimum wage law entirely. That is the only thing that can save our great nation. yeah! I know! I stand alone on knowing this fact.

SIRMANS LOG: 4 AUGUST 2013, 2210 HOURS.

A Freddie L. Sirmans quote:
Abolishing the minimum wage law will drain the swamp. The swamp is where the welfare state beast lives. The swamp is where all of the anti-survival morality snatchers are coming from. The anti-survival morality snatchers are slowly taking over all of our souls.

TRIVIA NOTE:
Holiday Street in Valdosta, GA. is located within a few yards of where the home was located of the famous western gun fighter "Doc Holiday." It was where he lived as a teenager before going to dental school and heading out west.

WISDOM NOTE:
No one can achieve the great supernatural wisdom that I have without paying an awesome price to survive, and in my case it has been a knockout drag out mentally battle to

survive practically all of my life. Still, I have no monopoly on pain or struggle.

PASSING THOUGHT:

If abolishing the minimum wage law is not going to be taken seriously by the USA I'm beginning to suspect the Mayan calendar may not be very far off the mark after all.

Economic ignorance galore abounds, that's what it is: This caller made a profound statement on TV this morning, his view was that the tax payers were the source of all government funding. Wow! This guy was on to something and he knew more than most, but, he was wrong. Okay, let's do a walk through.

Government funding does come from the tax payers, but, where do the tax payers get their money? All tax payers get their money from their employers or some type of business transaction, period. It goes further; still we haven't arrived at the source of all government funding.

The real source is what gives in my view the shallow minded liberals a problem and is the reason liberals with total power is so dangerous to freedom and democracy. The true answer is: All government funding comes from some type of private business profit.

It is all about profit, profit, and more profit and that can come only from private enterprise. The government can only tax profit or the result of some type of profit, otherwise it cannot survive, period.

In general the shallow minded liberals hate the word profit and too a lesser degree hate business people. The welfare state is the reason the man or woman on the street has no concept of the true role of profit except personally having cash in hand.

You can't get blood out of a turnip and government can't tax where no profit is made. Look at Detroit and California all bastions of liberalism. Unless the minimum wage law is abolished to break the liberal death choke hold on the throat of America that will be the picture of the whole country. God save America!

Liberals are who they are and they love America as much as I do even if I do think they are shallow. It is not entirely the liberals fault, it is the system that got us in our dire situation and only the system can save us, that is why the minimum wage law must be abolished entirely.

Everyone wants to make more money and no one want to make less when we can't make ends meet as it is. But, my great supernatural wisdom know abolishing the minimum wage law is the only way out for the USA to survive, period.

If not for the minimum wage law the cost of living for the poor and everyone would drop so they could pay their own food and doctor bills especially with nuclear family help. But, then the government would lose its God like power as a super provider.

The minimum wage law is blocking everything we buy from dropping down where the poor can pay out of pocket like a free market has always worked before the "New deal." It is the buying power of money that truly matters, not some inflated worthless high number. **SIRMANS LOG: 24 JUNE 2013, 1123 HOURS.**

USA CRIMINAL JUSTICE SYSTEM IS NOT PERFECT BUT STILL THE WORLDS BEST.
Let me try to shine some light on this. In the USA we have an adversarial

criminal justice system which is not perfect but overall still the fairest known to man.

The prosecutor tries everything it can to win the case and on the other hand the Defense tries everything it can to prevent losing the case. Well. Most of the time somewhere in the middle justice will be realized but not always.

The system is not about emotions, right or wrong, or feelings because then justice would always be one-sided and never balanced. However, Joe six-pack and most laymen's believe that if you commit the first wrong and a tragedy result the blame is on you, period.

Sure, Christianity allows mercy and forgiveness, but, when you set a tragedy in motion you can't expect a pat on the back and hero worshiping unless racial bias is involved.

The biggest loser in this whole thing could end up being the Democratic Party. That is because if the blacks stay pissed-off enough they may stay home during the mid term election next year.

This is a dire survival situation in the eyes of most blacks; yet, I for one believe there is some un-necessary stoking of this highly emotional matter. Cooler and calmer heads is what's needed, instead of a lot of flamboyant rhetoric that fans the flames.

SIRMANS LOG: Updated 17 JULY 2013, 1103 HOURS.

OK:
I have commented on this tragedy, so I might as well go whole hog and say what I really feel about the overall African American situation. But, this is an emotional charged issue and I know that truth and reasoning's won't win me a popularity contest.

Sure, there is racialism in America, always has been and always will be. However, racialism may be an obstacle but that is not what is holding African Americans back or down, especially in this day and time. Before the welfare state came along African Americans faced slavery and a far harsher climate than today, Yet, still owned far more.

I'm going to cut right through the chase and strike right at the heart of the African American community problem. I think as a rule African Americans still has a slavery dependency mentality and don't feel entirely responsible for their own survival as a race.

African Americans are stereotyped as violent prone, criminal prone, likely to lower property values, and bring social baggage in most cases. Whoa, anybody thinking that must be a racialist, maybe or maybe not.

What is never said or admitted is every stereotype has a truth foundation. And you can't dismiss a stereotype by ignoring it and making excuses for bad behavior. When bad behavior is excused and ignored it will reflect on the entire race. And it is not facing reality to think otherwise.

Yet, ignoring that fact is typical liberal behavior. By the African American leadership not taking responsibility for our own behavior as a race causes us all to suffer the consequences of being stereotyped in a bad way. Jealousy, envy, sibling rivalry, and a host of negative emotions come along with having a dependent mentality.

Whereas one with an independent mentality tends to soars above the negative stuff, and will accept total responsibility for himself, his race, and his country. As to jobs, the white man is expected to supply all of the jobs.

There are plenty of African Americans with plenty of money, why shouldn't blacks as race be expected to supply more of their own jobs to their community.

I could go on and on but I think I made my point; we need to get a grip and feel totally responsible. I don't have the answer but I do know before the welfare state no one feared black men. Before you can solve a problem you first must admit you have a problem.

I say the African American community has a problem facing up to the truth. And I think it boils down to taking total responsibility for one's own survival. The surest way to cure dependency is to have the props and crutches taken away, but that can't happen as long as we have a welfare state.

Denying truth is the same as denying reality. And that is exactly what African

Americans leadership and spiritual leaders have been doing for years concerning black crime. I have no power to stop bad behavior or crime, but, you can bet your bottom dollar that I will never condone it or make excuses for it no matter who does it.

Folks, I have no power to change anything, I'm just thankful I can still write and say what I believe. God Bless America.

SIRMANS LOG: 19 JULY 2013, 2234 HOURS

THE END

FREDDIE L SIRMANS SR. IS FROM VALDOSTA, GEORGIA USA. VALDOSTA, GA. IS THE CHILDHOOD HOME OF THE FAMOUS WESTERN GUN FIGHTER "DOC" HOLIDAY.

FREDDIE L SIRMANS SR. WEBSITE: FLSirmans.com